GW00863114

THE WAY OF THE MUSLIM

THE WAY OF THE MUSLIM

by

DR. MUHAMMAD IQBAL

illustrated by

EDWARD MORTELMANS

HULTON EDUCATIONAL

ISBN 0 7175 0632 0

First published 1973
Reprinted 1975
Reprinted 1977
Reprinted 1979
Reprinted 1983

HULTON EDUCATIONAL PUBLICATIONS LTD.
Raans Road, Amersham, Bucks

Printed in Hong Kong by Wing King Tong Co Ltd

CONTENTS

Acknowledgements

The author wishes to thank E.G. Davies, M.A., B.D., M.Phil., Lecturer, State Hospital, Carstairs, Lanarkshire and Mary Newman, School Teacher, Huddersfield, for helpful advice and discussion.

Bab Zuwela, Cairo

The Muslims and the Mosques

The Taj Mahal is one of the Seven Wonders of the World. It is in Agra, a place in India, and was built in 1653 by the Moghul Emperor Shah Jahan in memory of his wife Mumtaz Mahal, whom he loved dearly. This tomb, which some people think is the most beautiful building in the world, has the great domes and high minarets that are found on Muslim places of worship, the mosques, or 'masjid' like the Bab Zuwela Mosque in Cairo.

In the mosques Muslims pray to Allah, which is their name for God. A Muslim may worship Allah at home, or anywhere, but the mosques are regarded as the special places of prayer. This is why they are so beautiful. All mosques face Mecca in Saudi Arabia and look like the Masjid-al-Nabvi, the Prophet Muhammad's mosque in Medina, Saudi Arabia, built in 622.

Because Muslims must worship only God, you will not see any images representing God, nor any statues or pictures of the Prophet and his followers. However, the walls of the mosques are decorated with many bright floral patterns, tapestries, engravings, Arabic writings and pictures of landscapes. Five times a day Muslims may gather there for prayers. Some parts of the mosque are used as schoolrooms, where children are taught by the Imam, or religious leader, about the Muslim faith and learn to read and recite the Arabic language.

The Kaaba in Mecca

This large cube-shaped building called the Kaaba is said to have been built originally by the Prophet Abraham. This is the same Abraham of whom we read in the Old Testament, and he is one of the prophets of the Muslim faith. The Kaaba was later rebuilt by the Prophet Muhammad and Muslims believe that, although Allah is everywhere, this is His special House on Earth. For this reason, thousands of Muslims of many different races visit the Holy Shrine every year. Both men and women have their heads shaved and are dressed in two sheets of white cloth. They repeat prayers many times, walk round the Kaaba and perform a large number of other religious rites.

A sheep, goat, cow or camel is sacrificed in token of the Muslim belief that Ishmael, the Prophet Abraham's son, was almost killed in order to please God whom he loved above all things. Every year, on the day of 'Eid-al-Adha' in the month of Dhil-Hajjah of the Muslim lunar calendar, all Muslims celebrate this event in the same way. It is one of the great days of rejoicing, especially for Muslim children, who receive gifts, just as Christian children do at Christmas time.

The Kaaba in Mecca

The Teaching of the Prophet Muhammad

Allah is regarded as the Creator and the Controller of all natural things. From time to time, Allah sent prophets to all the nations and tribes of the Arab world and also to other lands in the Mediterranean, to Africa, the Middle East, Asia and beyond. These prophets taught people to do good and to shun evil deeds. Some of them left their teachings in the form of books.

Those who follow the teachings of the Prophet Muhammad are called Muslims because they follow the religion of Islam, which means "submission to the Will of God", as written down in the Holy Qur'an. This book, whose name means "reading", is honoured and handled with great care. It is a collection of Allah's words which were brought to the Prophet Muhammad by the Angel Gabriel.

The first thing that every Muslim child learns from the Qur'an is known as the Kalimah and it is expressed in these words: "There is only one God and Muhammad is the last of the prophets". The Qur'an also tells of the Scrolls of Abraham, the Psalms of David, the

The Kalimah

Torah of Moses and the Testament of Jesus. Another book, called ‘Hadith’, which means “sayings”, is made up of words of advice and guidance spoken by Muhammad, and it helps to explain the Qur’an and to throw light on the life of the Prophet.

Some of the beliefs which Muslims hold, in common with people of other religions, are those about heaven and hell, about the Day of Judgement and life after death, and about angels.

The Birth of Muhammad

On the morning of Monday, 20th April 571, a child was born to Amina, the wife of Abdullah, son of Abdul Mutlib, the head of the famous Quraysh tribe in Mecca and a descendant of the Prophet Abraham. She called the boy Muhammad. Even before his birth, according to legend, Amina had been given strange insights into the future. In one story she heard a voice telling her that she was to have a child who would be the lord of the people. When he was born she was to say "I shall put him into the care of God and call him Muhammad". Another story describes how a light shone from Amina's body, and with its aid she could see places hundreds of miles away. It is also told how, at this time, the people of Mecca were suffering from famine and disease. Yet, as soon as the baby Muhammad was born, there suddenly came rain, to put an end to the drought and hunger, and all the people recovered from their sickness and were well again.

Unfortunately, Muhammad's father had died only a few days before his son's birth. His mother Amina decided to follow the custom of hiring a foster-mother for her baby, and she put him into the care of a woman called Halima, who also had a young son of her own to

Peasants rejoicing over rain at Muhammad's birth

feed. She looked after him well and both the babies thrived. After two years, however, she began to worry about the little boy whom she had taken into her family. One day her own son came running to her with a frightening tale that he thought he had seen two men in white gowns tearing at Muhammad's stomach. Halima and her husband went to Muhammad and he told them the same story. They were very alarmed, and thought he might be possessed by demons, something in which people often believed in those days. They went to see Amina, his mother, about their fears but she reassured them, and Muhammad stayed with the family for another two years.

Then, when Muhammad was six years old, his mother died. He was taken care of by his grandfather, who died two years later. Afterwards, at the age of eight, he came under the care of his uncle Abu Talib.

Muhammad, Shepherd and Trader

Muhammad's uncle was very kind to the young boy, who was thoughtful and well behaved. He did not ask for much and was never any trouble. He looked after his uncle's sheep and was so reliable that other people also entrusted him with their sheep. In this way he was able to earn a small amount of money towards his keep.

Abu Talib's business took him to many far-off places. Once when he was setting out for Syria, Muhammad asked if he could go with him. His uncle agreed. As they travelled through Basra, in Iraq, they came across a Christian monk, Bahira, who foretold that Muhammad would become the greatest prophet of Allah, saying "Verily, I saw the trees and everything else bowing down before Muhammad and his followers as they climbed down the mountain". He also pointed to the sign of prophethood on the boy's back.

Throughout his childhood, Muhammad watched and learnt a great deal about trading until he too became a very clever business man. He came to be known as 'Sadiq', the truthful one, and 'Amin', the trustworthy.

Angel Gabriel with scroll outside Muhammad's cave

Muhammad Marries Khadijah

It was not long before Khadijah, a wealthy Meccan widow, heard about Muhammad's honesty and business skill. She handed over the management of her business affairs to the young man, and soon Muhammad married Khadijah. He was twenty-five and she was forty.

Although Khadijah was so much older than Muhammad, she had several children, but some of them died at an early age. Only the descendants of one daughter, Fatimah, still survive today.

Muhammad and Khadijah were very happy together and showed great kindness and affection, not only between themselves, but also to others. They gave away most of their property to the sick and poor and set free all Khadijah's slaves. This was an astonishing thing to do at a time when riches were admired above all things, and slaves were treated very harshly.

The Divine Call

For years, Muhammad meditated in the Cave of Hira which overlooked the Kaaba. He had many strange and puzzling dreams, but in the course of time they all came true. He was forty years old when the Angel Gabriel appeared to him in the cave as he meditated. The angel held out a silk parchment to him and commanded him to read the words written there. Muhammad explained that this was impossible, as he did not know how to read and write. Again the angel commanded him to read. To his surprise, Muhammad found that he could read. The words on the parchment were:

"Read: In the name of thy Lord who createth...
man from a clot.
Read: And thy Lord is the most Bounteous,
who teacheth by the pen,
teacheth man what he knew not."

Muhammad went home amazed. As always, he told his wife what had happened. She told him that because he was a good, honest and compassionate man this mysterious event must be the work of God, and not the devil. Khadijah's cousin, Waraqa, a Christian monk, agreed with her. He believed that Muhammad had a "divine call" to the prophethood.

This was, in fact, the first of a series of revelations which were told to Muhammad's companions and later these revelations were written down, exactly as they happened, to form the Holy Qur'an.

Qur'an on pedestal

Enemies of the Prophet

At first, Muhammad was laughed at by almost everyone. Only a handful of people supported him and these were Khadijah, Zaid, who was a freed slave whom Muhammad regarded as his own son, his young cousin Ali, and Abu Bakr, his faithful friend. Although Abu Talib loved his nephew dearly and would never have let him come to any harm, he did not share Muhammad's new faith. As chieftain of the powerful Quraysh family, he had to be very careful to observe the old ways and traditions.

In this Arab country in the seventh century, people were divided by their own greed and wickedness, and felt great fear in their hearts. They would pray to idols, and bury baby girls alive, having no respect at all for women. But Muhammad's new religion, which was gradually being revealed to him by God, began to change these ideas. It said that there must be dignity and equality for everyone, including women and slaves. Such teaching inspired some of the young men who heard it, and a small band of followers grew up. However, it was also a threat to the former way of life, to the people in power and the slave-owners. As a result, there were those who hated Islam and who were determined to get rid of Muhammad.

She swept dust over Muhammad

On one occasion he was almost strangled. There were many plots to kill him, but they failed. Dirt and stones were often thrown at him. It is said that one woman was in the habit of sweeping out the dust from her house all over Muhammad as he passed every day on his way to the mosque. He would greet her with a friendly 'Assalamu Alaikom', which means "peace be upon you". One day he discovered that the woman was very ill. Immediately he went into the house, looked after her and did the housework until she was well again. She was sorry for having behaved so badly, and became a follower of the new faith.

Not everyone, unfortunately, was converted so easily. The band of Muslims at last found that life was made unbearable for them, and they were forced to flee to the infertile valley of Shib Abi Talib. Many of them died of starvation. The survivors were eventually allowed to return to Mecca. The Meccans hoped that by this act of kindness they would persuade the Muslims to forget their religion, but the Muslims were determined to hold to their faith.

Muhammad Moves to Medina—The Beginning of the Islamic Calendar

When Muhammad's uncle Abu Talib died, ten years after the divine call, life became much more difficult for Muhammad's followers. It was a time of double sorrow for Muhammad, as Khadijah also died.

He decided to go to Medina to join Muslims there who had been converted to Islam during pilgrimages to the Kaaba. His followers were the first to depart. Soon after Muhammad had set off, accompanied by Abu Bakr, they were pursued by a group of Meccans. The two men were forced to hide in a cave. The horsemen approached the cave expecting to find the fugitives. Imagine their surprise when, on reaching the entrance, they found that a spider's web was stretched right across it, completely unbroken. There, too, was a pigeon comfortably settled on her nest, making it seem impossible that anyone could have passed that way or be hidden inside. Baffled, the Meccans turned back, and Muhammad and Abu Bakr were able to continue their journey to Medina in safety.

It was not for a long time, however, that the band of Muslims was allowed to worship in peace, and during this time many battles had to be fought to defend the new faith.

The Murderer is Forgiven

In Arabia at this time transport was chiefly by means of a camel caravan. Muhammad travelled this way on many occasions and many stories are told of his encounters.

On one occasion, in the burning heat of the mid-day sun, the caravan stopped to rest the camels. The Prophet lay down under a nearby tree. He went to sleep as soon as his head touched the ground.

Now among the travellers was a man who hated Muhammad and his teachings. As he saw the Prophet lying down he thought that this was a wonderful chance to kill him. Quickly he ran towards him and took out his sword. The Prophet woke up, just as the man was about to strike. His enemy said, "Muhammad, who can save you from me now?" The Prophet, who did not seem to be afraid, answered, "Allah, the one Almighty God will save me." The man was so surprised to find someone who did not fear death that he dropped his sword. At once the Prophet grabbed his attacker with one hand, picked up the sword with the other

Camel caravan resting

and said, "Tell me now, who will save you from me?" The man now saw that without faith he was lost, for he would surely die at the hands of Muhammad. How thankful he was when the Prophet allowed him to go free. The result was that this man became a devoted Muslim for the rest of his life.

Muhammad Returns to Mecca

In Medina, the Prophet began to encourage rich Muslims to help their poorer brethren, who would do what they could in return.

With the consent of all races—the Arabs, Jews, Christians and people of other religions—he established a city-state. He drew up a written constitution covering both religion and politics, defining the duties and rights of citizens and heads of state. There were laws about defence and foreign affairs, about how the community was to be organized and protected, and about religious freedom. Muhammad himself was elected the first governor.

He made many journeys to neighbouring tribes, making treaties which helped to prevent the constant attacks made by the Meccans on the property and lives of Muslims journeying to Medina.

In spite of growing friendship with other nations, Muhammad's life was still always in danger. The Meccans even demanded that he and his companions should be handed over to them, or expelled from Medina. At last they sent a powerful army which, although three times as great as the Muslim army which came to meet them, was miraculously defeated.

A year later, the Meccans, with an even larger army attacked again at Uhud but they were forced to return, neither side winning the battle. Meanwhile, the Prophet, by sending messages bearing his seal, was still in touch with neighbouring nations who were adopting Islam as their religion and who were beginning to look once more to Mecca as their spiritual home.

Seal of Muhammad

Leading an army of ten thousand, Muhammad overcame the Meccans more by surprise than by force. He ordered the idols in the Kaaba to be destroyed. Then he addressed the people, reminding them of their evil deeds, robbery and violence and asked, "Now what do you expect of me?" As they stood with heads lowered in shame and fear, he simply said, "May God pardon you: go in peace ... You are free." Only a few hours later, Mecca accepted the faith of Islam.

The Death of the Prophet

In the tenth year after the Hegira, as the Prophet's flight from Mecca is known, Muhammad went to Mecca for the Hajj, or pilgrimage. There he addressed 140,000 Muslims from many different parts of Arabia. He gave his most famous sermon which clearly set out all his teachings of Islam. On returning to Medina he became ill and within a few weeks he died. The year was 632.

Out of chaos and wickedness he had created both a religion devoted to one God, and a well-disciplined state. He had given peace in place of continual war. He had guaranteed a new system of law and justice for all. He allowed people to worship as they pleased: he took care of the poor and decreed that the ruler should not own the wealth which belonged to the people. The noble leader of an inspiring faith, he died poor in wordly goods, but rich in friends and spiritual comfort. His tomb is till today visited by thousands of Muslim pilgrims every year.

Islam at the time of Muhammad

The Spread of Islam

With the death of Muhammad, the Muslims had lost their great leader. The enemies of Islam hoped that the followers of the new religion would soon give up their faith. Not only was it necessary that the new leaders should keep alive their memory of the Prophet and their reverence for the Holy Book, but also that they should be able to rule the growing Muslim Empire justly and firmly in the face of threatened plots and attacks from outside.

The first four Caliphs, which means successors, of Islam were Abu Bakr, Umar, Uthman and Ali, known as The Rashidins. They were men of outstanding character. Unselfish, tolerant, well-versed in the scriptures, they lived simple lives and managed to rule wisely over their ever-widening kingdoms. Throughout this period Islam spread to Persia, Byzantium, Northern India and North Africa.

When Uthman was an old man of eighty, he was asked to abdicate by men who wanted to replace

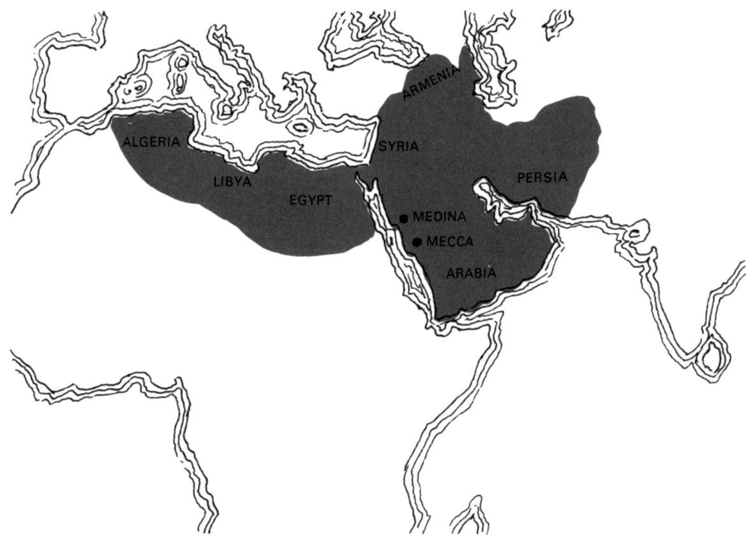

Spread of Islam under Abu Bakr, Umar and Uthman

him as Caliph. He refused, and was murdered. Ali succeeded him, but he too was put to death in 661. The death of Ali marked an important change in the lives of the Muslim people. The Rashidins had upheld the spirit of the Prophet and the word of God.

Ali's son Hassan was chosen as the next Caliph, but he resigned the position. There was now much disagreement among the Muslims, and many of them, of the Sunni sect, turned to Muawiya, the governor of Syria. He took the title of Prince of the Believers and became the leader of the faith. Although he was a good ruler, some Muslims disagreed with his choice of his own son Yazid as the next Caliph. Those who disliked Yazid, therefore, settled in Persia and called themselves 'shi'ites'.

When Muawiya became the fifth Caliph a new Umayyad Dynasty, or line of rulers, began. He set up his capital in Damascus. In these green and pleasant lands, far from the dust and sand around Medina and Mecca, Muawiya allowed non-believers to govern his realm. At this time Muslim armies were marching forward through Spain to France. But at home the Caliph and his followers were living lives of luxury and ease and they began to lose touch with the Muslim people. This contact was something that the Prophet and the first four Caliphs had always tried very hard to maintain.

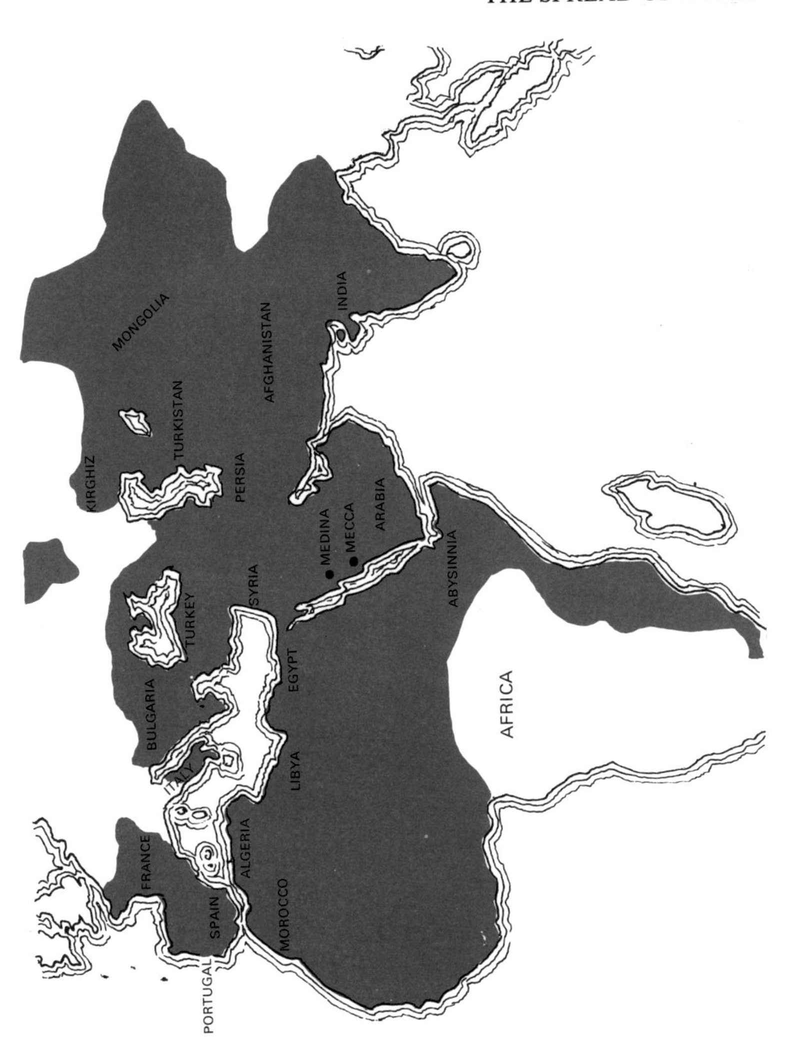

Muslim Empire at its height

One hundred years after Muhammad's death, the Muslim army was finally defeated in France. The soldiers began to lose hope. Under the rule of weak Caliphs, revolts broke out in Central Asia, Persia and Africa. Though they remained in Spain until 1492 the weak Umayyad rulers were overthrown in 747 by descendants of Al-Abbas, an uncle of Muhammad.

The Abbasid Dynasty was established in Persia. Baghdad became the new capital city, a great cultural centre. The most famous Caliph of this period was Harun-al-Rashid, whose rule is regarded by Muslims as the golden era of Muslim history. After that the Muslim Empire gradually split up into independent states.

In 910, Cairo became the capital of Egypt. Then, in the eleventh and thirteenth centuries came the Christian crusades. They did not achieve very much, apart from a worsening of relations between the Muslims and Christians, who now distrusted and hated one another. You can find out more about the famous men of this period—King Richard the Lionheart and Caliph Saladin the Just.

It was the Mongol-Tartar invasions in 1258 and the complete destruction of Baghdad by Hulagu, the grandson of Ghenghiz Khan, that ended the power of the Abbasid Dynasty, which had already begun to lead the way in knowledge and learning which later spread to Europe and helped to produce the Renaissance. Throughout this period, Muslims had translated the great works of the Ancient Greek, Indian and Persian civilisations, which led them to develop their own ideas in the fields of philosophy, medicine, mathematics, history, astronomy, music and architecture. Much of this work has formed the basis of knowledge still in use today. Sea and land travel led to the drawing up of accurate maps and geography books. Chemical research, almost unknown before, led to the first known school of Pharmacy. In Cordova, in Spain, Spanish Muslims, or Moors, established a university for scholars from all over the world, with a library of 400,000 books.

In the fourteenth century, Timur the Lame, or Tamerlane, a soldier, patron of the arts and a devout Muslim, captured Northern India, Afghanistan, Persia and Syria. In 1526 Muslim Turks under Sultan Suliman the Magnificent, defeated the Hungarians and were ready to march on Vienna. In the same year, the Mongols under Baber, a Muslim convert, founded the Moghul Empire in India, Russia and China. By 1900 nearly all Muslims except in China and the Turkish Empire were under British, French or Dutch Christian rule.

Today Islam is spreading once more, especially in Africa, and it can claim over 500-600 million followers of the faith.

The Five Pillars of Islam

It is the duty of all Muslims to try to find out as much as possible about the teachings of Islam, to believe and carry out these teachings to the best of their ability. Before anyone can truly call himself a Muslim he must perform five acts of faith which form the basis of the Islamic religion.

The first of these is the *Kalimah,* and anyone who recites and believes it may become a Muslim. It is the keystone to Islam, and reveals that God alone is worthy of worship and that Muhammad brought God's final message to the earth. It is God's truth and therefore must be believed.

The second pillar of faith is *Salat,* the saying of prayers five times a day, before sunrise, in the early afternoon, late afternoon, sunset and two hours afterwards. It reminds the Muslim that he is answerable to God alone for his words and deeds. He is commanded to pray in a special way and at regular times during the day, so that all Muslims, wherever they may be, can pray together with a united voice, all facing in the same direction and looking towards the Kaaba in Mecca. Before the act of prayer may take place, a Muslim must wash his hands, face and feet—this

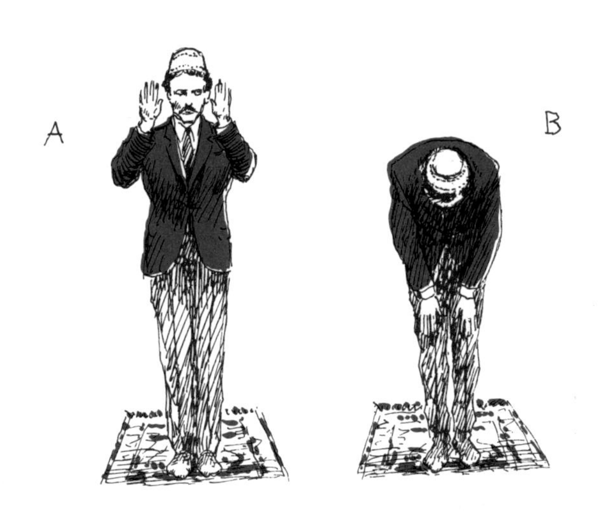

A. Commencement of prayer B. The bow

is known as 'Wazu'—and enter the prayer room barefoot. Worship, spoken in Arabic, consists of prayers and recitations from the Qur'an, and there are various special positions in which it must be done. Standing with hands raised to his ears, he recites 'Allah-o-Akbar—God is Great. Then, with arms folded across his chest, he repeats more prayers from the Qur'an from memory, before bowing from the waist, still reciting, and afterwards prostrating himself on the floor. This whole act is repeated two or three times. At various points in the service, extra recitations may be included. The Qur'an advises women to pray at home, but men are encouraged to gather at the mosque, where they are summoned by the Muezzin who chants the Call to Prayers from the top of the minaret at the exact time.

Friday is a special day for Muslims, and many people make an extra effort to attend the mosque where they will be welcomed by the Imam, or leader who, having learnt the whole or many parts of the Qur'an by heart, is able to lead the congregation in their act of worship. Women also attend the mosque on a Friday, which is a general holiday in Islamic countries.

The third pillar of faith is *Zakat,* which makes it a rule that one-fortieth of a Muslim's wealth must be given every year to the poor. It reminds him that all gifts and talents are given by God, and if others are born less fortunate and less able to provide for themselves, then it is the duty of Muslims to help them. Giving more than the required amount brings extra peace and joy to the hearts of men.

Fasting is the fourth pillar. During the lunar month of *Ramadhan,* a Muslim should not eat, drink or indulge in any pleasures between the hours of sunrise and sunset. He must do nothing sinful and think no evil thoughts. It is a great test of self-control. At the end of the month there is great rejoicing and feasting for three days. On the first day of the following month the major religious festival called 'Eid-al-Fitr' falls. Children are given new clothes and other gifts, and families invite one another to their houses.

As the lunar year (measured by the moon) is shorter by ten or eleven days than the solar year (measured by the sun) the lunar months are not fixed to the seasons, but gradually move through them. Because of this, fasting will take place sometimes in winter and sometimes in summer, at different periods in one person's lifetime.

The fifth and last pillar of faith is the *Hajj,* or pilgrimage to Mecca. To go there at least once during their lives is the great desire of all Muslims, although it is not compulsory for those who cannot afford it. There is a story of a man in Persia who had saved for many years to go on the Hajj. One day he saw a woman who

A. The prostration (Sijda) B. Finishing salute

was so poor that she had had to cook a chicken which had not been killed in the approved way, but had died naturally. He was so sorry for her that he gave her food and money. By now, however, he had not enough money to travel to Mecca, so he told his friends that he was ill and would follow later. Not surprisingly, he did not go at all. Yet when his friends returned they congratulated him on his Hajj. The man explained to them that he had not been. His friends only smiled and told him that they had seen him several times, and in a vision Allah had told them that he had made a wonderful pilgrimage. The Hajj is a time when the pilgrims are more keenly aware of a feeling of nearness to God and his Prophet.

These five pillars, then, are what the Prophet called "the foundation of Islam". They give Muslims the strength and desire to carry out many other religious duties.

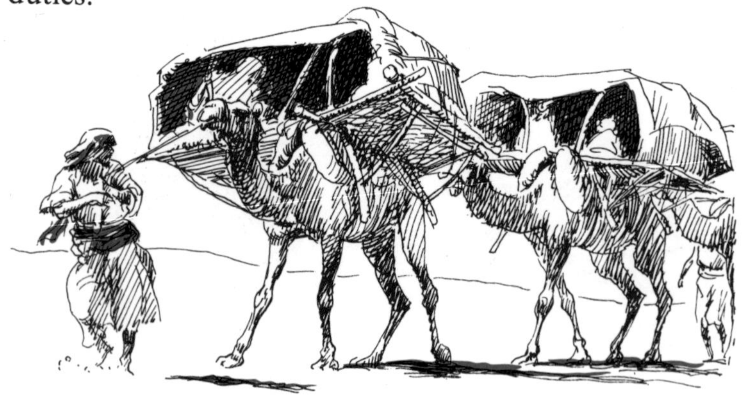

Muslim Ideals

A devout Muslim has certain ideals that he must remember, not only during prayers and worship, but at all times. The first is to love God, the Prophet Muhammad and the Islamic faith above all things. Indeed, the Qur'an tells him in Chapter 62, Verse 9, "O ye who believe! Let not your riches or your children divert you from the remembrance of God."

Then, too, he has a duty to show others how to become a good Muslim. He must also remain firm and true to God's faith at all times and in all circumstances. Another ideal is that of 'Jehad', which means doing everything possible by thought and deed to uphold and keep alive the way of Islam and obedience to God. This, he considers, is the best and truest way of life.

Yet other principles are those of 'Dhikr' whereby he must think about God all the time, and 'Tauba' which demands repentance for wrongdoing.

The Character of a Muslim

Every Muslim's duty is to seek knowledge and use all the gifts given to him by God. He must show good manners, truthfulness, justice, forgiveness, self-restraint, tenderness, humility, sincerity, courage and strength. He should be gentle in his speech, patient and worthy of trust. He should esteem cleanliness, as both healthy and righteous.

Here are some of the particular characteristics a good Muslim should try to develop. The first is piety and it may only be achieved by following the Divine Commandments conscientiously, and carefully avoiding wicked or shameful acts. "Nearest and dearest to me are those who possess the virtue of piety no matter what race or nationality they belong to or which country they live in." Honesty is also required in all things, especially in business. In the words of the Qur'an, "O ye who believe! Eat not up each other's property by unfair and dishonest means."

Good social conduct is very important. This means respecting the rights of everyone, including parents, husband, wife, children, relatives, neighbours, the poor and the weak. One should be tolerant of non-Muslims, without imitating their ways of life. Here

Pakistani Muslims washing in the river

is some advice from the Qur'an: " ... show kindness to your parents whether one or both of them attain old age with thee; and say not to them 'Fie!' neither reproach them — but speak to them both with respectful speech — and defer humbly to them out of tenderness ..."

The Hadith also has these words of wisdom: "He is the most perfect believer who is perfect in his manners and most affectionate towards his wife and children"; "He is not a Muslim who eats his fill and lets his neighbour go hungry."; "For God loves those who are patient and persevering."; "Show kindness, and kindness will be shown to you: forgive and you will be forgiven."

If a Muslim strives for these characteristics he will be led to a greater understanding of God and a place in the life hereafter. If he dies in the faith, it will be a great honour. Martyrs are not thought of as dead people. A special life is given to them in the life hereafter, where they receive wonderful favours and blessings from their Lord.

Here now are the sins that Muslims must not commit. They are murder, suicide, adultery, robbery and slander. Other forbidden things include the destruction or imprisonment of living creatures and plants without good reason or purpose, the drinking of alcohol and the eating of pork, or meat that is not ritually killed, or blood. It is also sinful to gamble or to take part in lotteries and betting. Cheating and forgery are wrong, and so too are the giving or taking of bribes.

Muslims are advised to lend money without interest, not to gossip; not to lead an idle life, to avoid crude forms of entertainment, and not to fight among themselves.

Life After Death

The Muslim learns from the Holy Qur'an that after death, a person's soul lives on. It moves from this material world into a "waiting state" called 'Barzakh'. Here it will be called to answer questions put by angels. A true believer is told that he will live in peace and happiness until the Last Day. The unbeliever will be punished until that day. On the Last Day, a time known only to God, the material world will be completely destroyed by Him. Then he will raise up all men to account for their lives on earth. In this Great Reckoning, those who are worthy will go to Paradise; those who are guilty will go to Hell.

In Paradise, or Heaven, souls will find everlasting happiness with no worries or pain. Those in Hell will know only misery and despair.

The Sufis or the Muslim Mystics

It is said that Malik bin Dinar was once travelling by boat but found he had not the price of the fare, one dinar. The owner of the boat began to beat him.

Fish with dinar in mouths

He was about to throw him overboard, when several fish, each holding a dinar in its mouth, came out of the water. Malik took one of the coins and gave it to the boatman who fell astounded at Malik's feet. Malik then stepped on to the water and walked away over the river.

You may well say that this was a man with a mysterious power. It is one of the many stories about, not only Malik, but many of the great Muslim mystics called Sufis. They are so called because they wear garments of wool, for which the Arabic name is 'Suf'.

Sufis are people who live their lives according to that of the Prophet Muhammad and devote their entire life to God in such a way that they become much nearer to Him than any ordinary person. Because of their constant love of God, unceasing trust in God, their abandonment of material goods and attainment of spiritual enlightenment through constant reading of the Qur'an, they are able to do things which most of us could not dream of doing.

They are thought to have great insight into the future and to be able to perform miracles such as curing the sick, providing food as though by magic and speaking to birds and beasts, and even to the dead. Because of these powers they are told to be careful not to use their knowledge wrongly, and to remember that whatever God gives He can also take away.

The writings and poetry of the Sufis are among the most wonderful works in Islamic literature. Of these, perhaps the most famous are the works of Al Ghazzali, Rumi and Umar Khayyam.

Religious Ceremonies and Customs

When a child is born into a Muslim family, the first words he or she hears are the *Aadhan* in the right ear and the *Iqaamah* in the left ear. Both are calls to worship God and love Muhammad as his Prophet. Soon after birth, the head is completely shaved, partly for health reasons, and partly to make the hair grow thicker. The hair which is removed is weighed and this same weight in money is given to the poor. If the baby is a boy he will be circumcised at an early age.

Babies are given names belonging to Muhammad and his family, and any of the ninety-nine personal names for God. As all Muslims are brothers and sisters in Islam, surnames or tribal names are not encouraged. This tends to cause problems in modern societies where people's names have to be registered for official purposes.

Soon after a child's fourth birthday, a family feast is held. On this occasion the child receives his or her first lesson, when verses about reading and writing are recited from the Qur'an. The boy or girl repeats each word. When the child is old enough, he or she is taught how to pray, and must gradually learn by heart certain verses from the Qur'an in Arabic.

Muslim bridegroom placing ring on bride's finger — modern

All Muslims are encouraged to marry. It is regarded as very natural that they should do so. Women may only marry Muslims, but men may marry Jews and Christians. Parents or older members of the family usually arrange the marriage, often taking a great deal of trouble to find a suitable partner for the son or daughter. The Qur'an does advise that the couple should have the right to agree or disagree to the match. This kind of arrangement may seem very strange to you, but it is a very old practice which has been followed by many races and creeds throughout the centuries.

The ceremony itself is very simple and takes place at the home of the bride. Bride and groom recite the appropriate verses from the Qur'an in front of the Imam and two male witnesses, one from each family. It is usually followed by much feasting and merriment. In the days when Muhammad was alive, men had many wives and often treated them very badly. The Qur'an tried to stop this practice by allowing a man to have up to four wives, but only one if he could not treat them all equally. The modern Muslim finds it much easier to look after one wife, and this practice is recommended by the Muslim jurists. Remarriage after the death of a partner, or after divorce, is allowed.

There are also special customs concerning the death of a Muslim. Before he dies he repeats the Kalimah, and so do those who are with him. The dead body is washed and cleaned, then wrapped in three sheets of cloth. The grave is a simple trench into which the body is placed with the head facing the Kaaba. Muslims are not expected to spend a lot of money on graves, but are encouraged to give that money to the poor.

In their day-to-day life Muslims must observe various customs. For instance, in their dress both men and women are expected to be modest. They should not emphasise the body and should wear clothes that discreetly cover it. For men, the Prophet recommended a beard, and he himself wore one.

Modesty of dress — Baluchi woman, Pathan man

On certain occasions a Muslim uses the word 'Bismillah', meaning "with the name of God". He does this before eating, before washing and before killing meat. Afterwards he says 'alhamdu lil-lah', or "God be thanked". Similarly, when Muslims meet one another they have a special greeting, 'Assalamu Alaikum', which means "peace be upon you".

Famous Muslims in the 20th Century

After the decline of the Muslim Empire, the people of Islam had little influence upon world affairs until the beginning of the twentieth century, when once again Muslim countries began to readjust and develop under new and strong leadership.

In Turkey, Mustafa Kemal Ataturk led his people in their fight for a modern republican nation. In India, a famous Muslim lawyer, Muhammad Ali Jinnah, founded the new state of Pakistan. Later, in Egypt, a new government, headed by General Muhammad Neguib, overthrew King Farouk. General Neguib was succeeded by Gamal Abdul Nasser. Perhaps you could find out more about these men and their countries. Other famous leaders of Muslim countries are King Hussein of Jordan, who is said to be descended from the Prophet, and King Faisal of Saudi Arabia.

In the twentieth century oil has brought wealth and prosperity to some Muslim countries of the Middle East.

Life in a Muslim Country Today

Riaz Ahmad is a Muslim boy. He lives in a village with his parents. He has one sister and a baby brother. His grandparents live with his family and his aunts and uncles live close by. Uncle helps Riaz's father in his general store. When he isn't at school, Riaz likes to help too. Sometimes he wanders through the dusty street stopping to look at the display of wares, gold and silver jewellery, wood carvings, copper pans, shoes and

Pathan village Elders discussing village business

carpets. A woman bargains with the shop-keeper over a piece of cloth, while another collects water from the well, though most houses in the village have running water and electricity now. Riaz wonders what life is like in the big city many miles away, where he hopes to study at the university one day. His uncle Ahmad is a doctor in one of the new hospitals and his wife teaches at a girls' school. Riaz knows that in the city everything is much bigger, newer and busier. There are wide roads, cars, flats, hotels, cinemas, parks, factories, offices, and people of all nationalities living there.

Here, in the village, life is still very simple but warm and friendly. Relatives and friends often have meals together. The main meal is usually eaten with rice and flat bread like pancakes. Pieces of bread are held in the right hand and are used to scoop up the curry. Sweet dishes or fresh fruit are eaten afterwards. The women sit together and talk about their sewing, shopping and children, while the men, usually in a separate room, discuss their work, politics and monetary matters such as the communal buying of a buffalo to add to the family's small stock of farm animals. Camels and goats are useful beasts, but buffaloes are valuable for pulling wagons and heavy loads. All the village is particularly happy, for soon Riaz's grandparents are to go on the Hajj.

Tomorrow, neither Riaz nor his sister will go to school. In the villages, towns and cities the shops will

Uncle Ahmad is a doctor

be closed and all work will stop. Everyone will be on holiday to celebrate the Prophet Muhammad's birthday. The villagers will go to the fair in a neighbouring town. There will be much fun and laughter. For Riaz, the happiest time will be watching the firework display, but for his parents and elders the most wonderful time will be in united prayer in the courtyard of the mosque. Uncle Ahmad and his wife will be praying too, with the millions of other Muslim city dwellers:

"The most blessed greetings, the purest and most sincere inclinations unto God. Peace be with thee, O Prophet, as well as the mercy of God and His

Riaz's happiest time will be watching the firework display

blessings. Peace be with us also, and the pious servants of the Lord. I attest that there is no god if not God himself, and I attest that Muhammad is His servant and Apostle."

Index